The Holy Ghost

A thought for each day of the year

Philip M. Hudson

Copyright 2019 by Philip M. Hudson.

Published 2019.

Printed in the United States of America.

All rights reserved.

No portion of this book may be reproduced, stored in a retrieval system, or transmitted in any form or by any means - electronic, mechanical, photocopy, recording, scanning, or other - except for brief quotations in critical reviews or articles, without the prior written permission of the author.

ISBN 978-1-950647-08-8

Illustrations - Google Images.

This book may be ordered from online bookstores.

Publishing Services by BookCrafters
Parker, Colorado.
www.bookcrafters.net

Table of Contents

Acknowledgements...i
Preface..v
Introduction...vii

A Thought For Each Day Of The Year..1
About The Author..367
By The Author..369
What More Can I Say?..373

Those who have
forsaken the world and
have faithfully embraced the
lifestyle of the Saints experience
nothing less than a spiritual heart
transplant. Therefore, anti-rejection
protocols must be followed after they
have received their new hearts. These
are orchestrated, in large part,
by the ministrations of
the Holy Ghost.

Acknowledgements

In this volume, I have attributed quotations to original authors whenever possible, as well as when I have editorialized their ideas. In many cases, however, my language will naturally reflect the teachings of leaders and members of The Church of Jesus Christ of Latter-day Saints.

The list of those who have contributed to this book is endless. As I have organized my own thoughts, I have realized how heavily I have borrowed from the towering examples of those who, over the years, have been my mystical mentors, my sensible chaperones, my spiritual guides, my surrogate saviors, my compassionate critics, and everything in between.

They are my avatars, manifestations of deity in bodily forms, my na'vi, the visionaries, who communicate with God on a level to which I can only aspire, and my tsaddik, whom I esteem as intuitive interpreters of biblical law and scripture. They are my divine teachers incarnate. They have offered listening ears, extended open arms. lifted my spirits, shown me the way, stretched my mind, reinforced my faith, strengthened my testimony, helped me to discover my wings, given immaterial support, provided of their means, emboldened me with words of encouragement, cheered me on with wise counsel, taught me humility, been there to steady me, soothed my troubled soul, stepped in to nurture me, led me to fountains of living water, wet my parched lips with inspired counsel, and bound up my wounds.

When I think of the influence of a multitude of angels thinly disguised as my family, friends, and peers, I remember the words of Sir Isaac Newton, who, when pressed to reveal the great secret behind his accomplishments, simply replied: "I stood on the shoulders of giants." Of course, at the end of the day, I alone am responsible for the content of this volume. But I hope my interpretations of principles and doctrine will cultivate your interest to dig deeper into the themes woven into this tapestry, by turning to the scriptures and seeking inspiration from the Spirit. My only goal is to help you to expand your insights into the telestial mile markers, the terrestrial truths, and the celestial guidelines that accompany each of us during our quest for enlightenment through the Spirit.

If we
will not listen
to the promptings of
the Holy Ghost, we cannot
reasonably expect to inherit
the glory of celestial realms;
especially if we have aforetime
been agreeable to only abide by
telestial or terrestrial principles
that put fewer demands upon
our discipleship.

It is the
Holy Ghost Who
motivates us to drag
our battered and beaten
bodies to the local chapter
of Weight Watchers, known
as The Church of Jesus
Christ of Latter-day
Saints.

Preface

I love to learn by reading the scriptures, and I often think of St. Hilary, who wrote in the third century: "Scripture consists not in what we read, but in what we understand." In each of the musings within this volume, I have consistently tried to find a scriptural foundation and a spiritual confirmation as I put my pen to paper.

I am continually reminded of Nephi's counsel to press forward with complete dedication and steadfastness, or confidence with a firm determination in Christ, having a perfect brightness of hope, or perfect faith, and charity, or a love of God and of all men. If we do this, feasting upon the word of Christ, or receiving strength and nourishment as we ponder the doctrines of the kingdom, and particularly the principles relating to the Holy Ghost, and as we then endure to the end in righteousness, we shall have eternal life, which is the greatest of God's gifts. (See 2 Nephi 31:20).

It is with love, then, that I extend to you the invitation to enjoy this omnibus of random thoughts. Embrace it at face value, and use its exhortations to seek the Spirit as a springboard to your own personal plateaus of discovery, as you are taught to move in the direction of your dreams.

If we
do not nurture
our relationship with
the Holy Ghost, but instead
hug the shadows, we will find
that we have consigned ourselves
to a spiritual vacuum, gasping
for life sustaining air while
we are only inches away
from rescue.

Introduction

If they are fortunate, novice quilters quickly learn a bit of wisdom from the Amish, who make some of the finest quilts in the world. On purpose, the Amish build mistakes into their projects, because they believe that any attempt on their part to design and produce a flawless creation would be a mockery of God, Who alone is perfect. The humility of the Amish makes me think of my own weak attempts to put the thoughts expressed in this omnibus to paper. In His infinite wisdom, God knows very well that I do not need to consciously plan on lacing my efforts with errors. That will come quite naturally, without the need for me to intentionally contribute to my short-comings.

Perhaps this serendipitous collection of musings will do little more than help to define quirks in my personality. Each of us is different, and many things, including our family and friends, the circumstances in which we find ourselves, the quality of our education, and our own personalities, inspire and mold our oral and written expressions. I would like to think that, in this text, all of these influences have been encouraging, affirmative, and constructive.

The reflections within this tome leave the door ajar for the reader, to allow shafts of the light of understanding to creep in. If, as I have expressed my thoughts, I mis-stated myself a few times, or flat-out got it wrong, I ask the patient indulgence and gentle correction of the reader.

Too often, I realize that my communications can be "carefully disguised with hypocrisy and glittering words," as Einstein put it. Although I do fancy myself a wordsmith, I have tried to avoid pedestrian expressions, idle language, and lazy scholarship. I do not pretend to be an authority on the Holy Ghost, inasmuch as I believe that we are all works in progress, but if you find the factual tone of a particular musing disengaging, the truth is that I typically experienced a deep personal involvement in my interpretation of the principles that illuminated its meaning.

In any event, when you open this volume, I hope you ponder these minute musings with as much enjoyment as I have experienced while creating them.

The Day of Judgment does not lie over a distant horizon, but is today. We speak, think, and act according to the celestial, terrestrial, or telestial laws that are before us. Just as a barometer is used to measure the direction in which the weather is headed, it is our relationship with the Spirit that helps us to remain aware of the direction we must follow if we hope to regain the shelter of our heavenly home.

The
Holy Ghost
elicits displays
of celestial energy.
As fire in the sky, the
air in the theater of life
is charged with electricity
that is the sum of the merger
of the universal encouragement
of the Light of Christ with the
pointed and providential
guidance provided by
the Spirit of God.

It is by our faith to see all the way to heaven that the power of the Spirit is released. It can penetrate the barriers that isolate us from the sum and the substance of our existence that, arguably, more accurately define reality.

The Holy Ghost disperses the powers of darkness from before us and causes the heavens to shake for our good. This is the Spirit of Justification.

The
focus of our faith
slips away gradually,
just as we lose the acuity
of our vision over time. Whether
it is the letter of the law or an eye
chart that is beyond our comprehension,
we become legally blind. Having eyes,
we cannot see what is clearly before
our faces, when we no longer
enjoy the guidance of
the Spirit.

The
disorder
of life roughly
hustles us further
and further from the
influence of the Spirit,
whose purpose is to guide
us away from that precipice
of destruction, and to lead us
to the secure sanctuary where
the stability of higher
laws abides.

It may be
the Spirit that
causes our blood to
run hot, reminiscent of
the microwave background
radiation from the creation
of our universe that occurred
billions of years ago, and of
the creation that occurred
in the Garden of Eden
that was not so very
long ago.

No
one has a
corner on the Spirit.
Each one of us has been
hard-wired to respond
to the invitation by
the Holy Ghost
to come unto
Christ.

The Holy Ghost is our mentor and our teacher. If we are good students, and have done our homework, He will reward us with an illumination of Gospel principles that bathes our minds and our spirits in a cascade of insight, intuition, inspiration and revelation.

Secular humanism and other ideologies that extoll the virtues of the intellect and demand tangible proof are incompatible with the Holy Ghost, destroying our faith, and diverting us from The Plan of Happiness whose execution centers upon nourishing the tender seeds of innocent faith in the revealed word of God. "Better had they ne'er been born, who reads to doubt, or reads to scorn." (Sir Walter Scott).

The
Holy Ghost
provides a shield
of protection against
the corrosive spatter of
perspiration cast off by the
destroyer, who pervasively and
persistently is working overtime to
damage our doctrinal defenses, dull
our spiritual sensitivities, diminish
our charitable capacity, deplete
our bountiful reservoirs of
sympathy, and destroy
our devotions.

The
Spirit charges
our vision with an
infinite perspective,
where we experience the
pulsing stream of insight,
intuition, inspiration, and
revelation whose mighty
flow has no spatial
and no temporal
boundary.

Faith is dead, without the accompanying work of repentance that is made possible by the Atonement. Even great faith lacks the power to save us from the unalterable demands of Justice. So that Mercy might prevail, God provided us with a Mediator, as well as with the Holy Ghost.

The
Holy Ghost has
the means to reset
our spiritual appestat
when we notice it is out
of whack and we find
ourselves indulging,
and even binge
eating, in
sin.

The
Holy
Ghost has
no spiritual,
spatial, or even
temporal limitation.
He can be experienced
at one and the same time
in the past, the present,
and the future; now
and forever.

As if they
were our spiritual
swaddling clothes, the
fabric of our faith that has
been woven into our coats
of many colors resonates
with intrinsic light that
radiates in a pulsing
stream from the
witness of the
Spirit.

Those who
enjoy spiritual
gifts have the image
of God engraven upon
their countenances. They
shall ascend into the hill of
the Lord. They shall stand in
His holy place to partake of the
divine nature, because they have
clean hands and pure hearts, and
have not lifted up their souls unto
vanity, nor sworn deceitfully.

When we invite the Holy Ghost to be Guru, Guide, and Governor, we don't allow ourselves to get in the thick of thin things. Instead, we establish an equilibrium that is centered far from the madding crowd, at a safe distance from the ego-filled minds of mediocre men. We are insulated from the clamor, the confusion, and the cares of the world, and enjoy a firmness that is unshakable.

Obstacles are
those terrifying
things we see when
we take our minds off
our goals. They loom large
with gratuitous significance. The
Spirit endows us with the vision to
see beyond these potential stumbling
blocks. It empowers us to rely upon
an expansive, creative engine for
positive change that is driven by
the Holy Ghost, to turn them
into stepping-stones that
pave the way to higher
achievement.

During our
journey of faith,
we use the talents we
have been given by the
Holy Ghost, for we know
that the woods would be
very quiet if no birds
sang except those
that sang
best.

At times, we may talk about the Gospel in superficial ways by retreating into insipid and colorless verbiage as an easy way out. We need to be careful that we do not steer a course for ourselves that drives away the Spirit with expressions that are offhand, dismissive, apologetic, or inconsiderate.

Those who have made the
effort to really get to know
the Holy Ghost have been able to
break free of "the influence of that
spirit which hath so strongly riveted
the creeds of the fathers, who have
inherited lies, upon the hearts of
the children, and filled the
world with confusion."
(D&C 123:7).

As we repent, we draw upon the magnificent power of all three members of the Godhead, so that we may become increasingly receptive to flashes of insight. We are cast off into streams of revelation that carry us along in the quickening currents of direct experience with our Heavenly Father, with Jesus Christ and with the Holy Ghost.

Spiritual neglect
in any degree requires
that we take drastic action.
The plastic surgery of repentance
is prompted by the Holy Ghost, and is
indicated if we expect to experience
a reversal of our fortunes, and if
we hope to restore the likeness
and image of God to
our countenances.

Paul was referring to the power of the Holy Ghost when he wrote: "Ye are manifestly declared to be the epistle of Christ ministered by us, written not with ink, but with the Spirit of the living God; (and not just) in tables of stone, but (also) in fleshy tables of the heart." (2 Corinthians 3:3).

When the Spirit no longer influences behavior, and when every man walketh in his own way, and after the image of his own god, the erosion of faith becomes inevitable, and will surely be followed by the chaotic crash of cultural cohesion and stability.

It makes no
difference if we
turn to the right or
to the left, because the
Spirit is always there. When
we lift our eyes to the heavens,
He is watching us from above. No
matter that we bear the weight of
sin or sorrow with downcast eyes;
He is always beneath us, to lift
us up and carry our burdens.
Each time we knock, He is
there to answer. If we
simply ask, He will
bless us beyond
measure.

The Lord
created the earth
as a testing center,
a learning laboratory, a
citadel of higher education,
a place where we would be given
all the tools that could conceivably
be necessary, beginning with the gift
of the Holy Ghost, to validate God's
faith in us, and to see if we might
muster an equivalent faith, to be
proven worthy of His trust.

We
are given
the gift of the
Holy Ghost after
our baptism, but often
we leave it undisturbed
in its original packaging,
forgetting that He is always
there to help us make the
most important, as well
as the less important,
decisions of our
lives.

The mortal ministry of Jesus Christ among the children of men may be the greatest miracle of all, but those who deny the Lord's divinity cannot be saved on His merits alone, because they have not generated faith with enough power to carry their progression onward. Only a profound attitude adjustment will jump-start their forward momentum along the pathway leading to the Kingdom of God.

The
Holy Ghost frees
us from incarceration
to confusion, hesitation,
doubt, ignorance, mistrust,
skepticism, suspicion,
uncertainty, and
worry.

Since there
is opposition in
all things, even as there
is faith, so must there also
be its worldly counterpart. In
our day, the grip of fear paralyzes
many of God's children. Today, more
than ever, we need the Holy Ghost. We
need the assurance of peace, that our
lives are moving in the direction
of our dreams, and that the
Atonement can help us
lasso our wagons
to the stars.

When we
encounter truth,
our sinews will resonate
with recognition. Ultimately,
every one who hearkens to
the voice of the Spirit will
eventually come unto
God, even our
Father.

The Holy Ghost helps us to have hands that become accustomed to lifting up those who need our support, and to be light upon our feet, that they might speedily carry us to those who have become imprisoned by poor choices, bad habits, or unfortunate circumstances.

The Holy Ghost
encourages us to
surrender our agency
to Christ, knowing that
it is a necessary and vital
step on our path of progress
that leads to an independence
from servitude to sin.

The Spirit permeates the heavens, but like dark matter, defies detection by even the most sophisticated and accurately calibrated instruments utilized by terrestrial scientists.

Without the guidance of the Holy Ghost, we risk becoming more comfortable with our own perception of truth than we are with His omniscience. We pit our own capacities against His priesthood power, our own paltry overtures against His almighty works, and our stubborn won't against His gentle will.

Guidance from the Holy Ghost should be centered on the revelations the Lord has given us that relate to our world, and not on mysteries that have not been revealed to us, may never be explained, or that just may not be pertinent to our current circumstances.

By using specifically authorized and sanctioned words that we speak when we feel the powerful influence of the Spirit, we exercise the faith to perform ordinances that range from baptisms to sealings in the temple.

We have
all experienced
peace in our minds
concerning matters that
we have taken before the
Lord, that are of great
personal importance.
How sweet it is, to
have the Spirit
to be with
us!

The baptism of
water qualifies us
for membership in the
Church, but it does not
guarantee the total spiritual
transformation of our nature
that is necessary if we hope to
regain the presence of God.
This immersion only comes
thru the baptism of fire
and the Holy Ghost.

The Holy Ghost spectacularly responds to our needs. With a clear vision, the Spirit see the clouds before before they appear on our horizons, and issues weather advisories.

The Holy Ghost protects us from a false sense of carnal security, as well as from indifferent complacency. He helps us to view our weaknesses in positively constructive ways, and encourages us to be aware of, and to take advantage of, our opportunities for personal improvement. He is constantly giving us new tools to use to better accomplish our mortal mission assignments.

When
we have developed
a relationship with the Holy
Ghost, we are liberated to enjoy
a peace of conscience, to receive
the blessings of the priesthood, to
serve others in more powerful and
significant ways, to resolutely work
toward our potential, to commune
with the Infinite, and to benefit
from all of the other blessings
of The Plan of Salvation, as
we move forward into
eternity.

As we
travel in
faith thru the
harsh wasteland
of Idumea, oases
will spring up in the
desert of life, to slake
our thirst with living water.
Our spiritual roots will have
become anchored within
the bedrock of faith
thru the witness
of the Holy
Ghost.

The
Spirt
probes us
for pliability.
It searches us for
submissiveness, and it
measures us for meekness.
These hone our humility even
as they elevate us to higher
states of energy.

Because the testimony of Jesus is the spirit of prophecy, the Holy Ghost becomes a facilitator who helps to bring others of God's children to the knowledge of His Plan, to their own independent testimony of the Savior, and to faith in His Atonement, just as He has done with those who are already members of the Church.

We fall back
upon the strength of the
Holy Ghost, when we wonder,
as did Paul: "O the depth of the
riches both of the wisdom and the
knowledge of God! How unsearchable
are his judgments, and his ways past
finding out! For who hath known
the mind of the Lord? Or who
hath been his counsellor?"
(Romans 11:33-34).

The
Spirit
teaches us
that we are
God's chosen
people, and that
we live within His
embrace, enjoying a
security that others do
not know. We experience
a peace which surpasses
our understanding.

In the not too
distant future, there
will come for each of us
a great and dreadful day when
we will be asked to stand and give
our sworn statement before God and
angels, who will depose the witness of
the Holy Ghost. On the issue of faith,
depending upon our answer, we will
be counted among the sheep or the
goats, and find ourselves on the
right hand of God, or on His
left hand. It all depends
on us, and on how we
have conducted
our lives.

Those who are physically past their prime can still faithfully endure to the end, as long as they continue to cultivate a relationship with the Holy Ghost. It may come as a consolation to realize that when we are over the hill, we really do pick up speed.

How we
respond to
the Holy Ghost
will either deify us,
or it will destroy us. It
will delineate our dreams,
and define our destiny. It
will ultimately determine
how, where, and with
whom we will spend
all of eternity.

If we want
to develop the
faith to choose the
harder right instead
of the easier wrong, we
will maintain unbridled
optimism, and we will be
consumed, as it were, by
the divine fire of the
Holy Ghost.

The Spirit carries us to the edge of eternity, to the very portals of heaven, where "forever" stands revealed in the mind bending panorama that lies before us.

The vast and expansive
influence of the Holy Ghost
has the capacity to become the
underlying element of a tapestry
whose design will be revealed, in
all its glory, as an expression of
our being when we attain the full
stature of our spirits. When our
nature finally corresponds to
the harmony of heaven, our
perfect frames will burst
free of the shackles of
our mortal clay, as
vibrant coats of
many colors.

The Spirit
drives forward
the Kingdom of God
on earth. Those who bear
the priesthood and sit in its
presiding quorums do not focus
their attention on rituals that are
empty or passive. Rather, they exercise
their keys of authority in a way that
empowers them to bind us to the
blessings of heaven by means of
covenants of action between
ourselves and the Lord.
In this way, everyone
is involved in the
process.

As we
nurture our
relationship with the
Holy Ghost, we realize how
heavily we have borrowed from
the towering examples of those who,
over the years, have been our mystical
mentors, our sensible chaperones, our
compassionate critics. our spiritual
guides, and our surrogate
saviors.

When cultural
collapse is imminent,
external controls are often
imposed to manipulate behavior;
to maintain at least a semblance
of societal steadiness. Our escalating
dependence on laws to regulate moral
discipline says something about us,
and about our critical need for
guidance from the Holy
Ghost.

While the Spirit encourages our development of personality traits that are in concordance with the symmetry of heaven, sin is harmful because it destroys our ability to nurture the equilibrium that is a defining characteristic of all those who inherit eternal life. It is in the nature of our Heavenly Father, His Son, and the Holy Ghost, that there is neither variableness, nor shadow of turning.

Timid souls who are cautiously hesitant and tentatively faithful don't consciously intend to lose intimacy with the Holy Ghost. It just fades away, like a slow leak in an automobile tire, and not as a blowout. But, it may often be traced back to the tendency to mischief that may have taken root during a time period of particularly intense vulnerability to the wiles of the Devil.

The Holy
Ghost asks us to
go the second mile, and
to focus our discipleship on
the commandment to be willing
to mourn with those who mourn,
and to comfort those that stand
in need, and to be witnesses of
God, wherever we may be,
for as long as we
shall live.

Those of
weak will, who
turn their back to the
promptings of the Spirit
will forfeit their motivation to
repent, although they may not even
be consciously aware of it. They lose
their focus, just as eyesight may be lost
over time. First they will squint, and then
they might hold the page a bit closer or a
little further away, compensating for their
inability to see clearly. It could be either
the printed page or their integrity that
they cannot read. But in the latter
case, without the clarity that is
provided by the Holy Ghost,
there is a compromise of
character crippling
proportion.

Sometimes
all too quickly, and
at other times agonizingly
slowly, those who have sold their
souls to the Devil for a mess of pottage
are dragged down to a hell on earth that
is of their own construction. Their bad habits
are the result of repetitively impulsive behaviors
that, in a rising tide of wickedness, continually
erode away at the foundations of agency. They
are fettered by the chains of compulsions. They
realize too late that unlimited freedom leads
to tyranny. The Holy Ghost has the power,
however, to lead them back along the
path of safety to the Atonement
and to the perfect law of
liberty.

The Holy Ghost
will always be waiting
in the wings, to apply His
soothing balm to bruised
egos, bitter feelings, and
battered birthrights, in
a brilliant display of
benevolence.

When we turn our
backs on the invitation
that has been extended by
the Holy Ghost to introduce us
to God, and we remain alienated
from Him by our spiritual death,
it is unavoidable that we must
eventually surrender to our
natural inclinations that
are carnal, sensual,
and devilish.

The Spirit points us in the direction of doctrine, so that when we encounter the principles of The Plan, we will respond to the truth with actions that have both the form and the substance of a godly walk, and that boldly testify of His power to save.

When
we express
ourselves through
positive and independent
action, the Holy Ghost will
introduce us to the exhilarating
emotion and feeling of freedom
from incarceration to sin that we
can only experience when we
have been obedient to a
Higher Power.

The
Holy Ghost
unshackles us
from the unpleasant
consequences of Justice.
Darkness is the conjoined twin
of misery, but the obedience of faith
frees us to embrace the truth, to make
intelligent choices, to perform purposefully,
to carry on convincingly, and to progress
persistently; in short, to rise above the
cares of the world through the
Atonement of Christ.

The world seeks change by exerting external controls, and fails miserably. The Spirit influences the inner vessel, and succeeds brilliantly. He does this by recalibrating our internal compass so that we will remain oriented toward the discipline of faith.

Our faith invites us to enjoy the influence of the Holy Ghost, Who, as a creative consultant, always stands ready to offer His constructive comments relating to our developing storyboard.

Belief is the mental nod to the truth of a precept or principle. But it lacks the moral element of responsibility that we call faith. Of those to whom much is given, however, much is expected. Our faith demands action that is supported and strengthened by the encouragement of the Holy Ghost. He is anxious to bear His witness of every good thing, but only if we take the initiative to exercise the faith to believe.

There is no
revelation where
there is no student,
and as long as we ask
the wrong questions, we
will be at odds with the
Spirit, with biblical faith,
and with revealed truth.
A rational mind cannot
hope to bridge the gap
that exists between
the secular and
the divine.

We are on the path that leads to celestial glory when we accept inspired direction from the Holy Ghost. Our progression is linked to faithful consistency in our discipleship.

We are
lucky to have
been blessed with
the gift of the Holy
Ghost, and to become
witnesses of His power. We
find redemption through the
grace of our God, and by the
shedding of Christ's blood,
which is in the covenant
of the Father unto the
remission of our sins.
We are consecrated
to become holy
and without
spot.

It is
our Father's
desire for each
of us to satisfy the
entrance requirements
for admittance into His
Kingdom. We could not be
blessed with a greater gift
to do so, than that of the
Spirit, Who is our willing
and capable Teacher.

The
Holy Ghost
puts the day to
day elements of The
Plan in perspective, that
we might more clearly be
able to distinguish the grey
toned obstacles that blockade
our way. These impediments to
progression will then stand out
in sharp contrast against the
polychromatic backdrop of
the design that God has
created for each
of us.

When we
have stockpiled
ample reserves in
our spiritual savings
accounts, when they are
nearing depletion, or even
if our accounts are overdrawn,
in every case we still receive
unexpected deposits from
our greatest benefactor,
who is the Holy
Ghost.

Our faith
blesses us with a
pure form of focus,
transforming our five
natural senses into something
wonderful, by a heaven-sent sixth
sense that defies description. Physical
and spiritual resources work in tandem
to compound each other, and to condition
us through the patience of faith, the miracle
of repentance, the diligence of baptism,
and the sweet spirit of the Holy Ghost,
to create an amalgamation that is
described as putting on
the whole armor
of God.

Wisdom leading to salvation comes in a breathtaking manifestation of the Spirit that is almost palpable in its effect upon us.

Sooner or later,
there is, for each of
us who has undergone a
spiritual heart transplant, a
moment in the sun, when the
steady light of understanding
illuminates our minds so that
the divine potential of the new
organs audibly beating in our
chests might be confirmed
by the powerful witness
of the Spirit.

The Holy
Ghost is able
to physically and
spiritually condition
us, that our backs might
become strong and sturdy
enough to brace us against
the brutal winds of adversity
and the wiles of the adversary.
He fortifies us, that our hearts
might become the repositories
of virtuous principles upon
which we may draw in
times of need.

Those of us
who have the faith to
become the beneficiaries
of the influence of the Holy
Ghost, have been touched by
angels, as we are moved by
compassion to walk in
the light of the
Lord.

Surely, we need
the wise counsel of
the Spirit now, as much
as we ever have, because we
have exponentially increased
the odds that we will destroy
ourselves if we are careless;
if we do not both carefully
and prayerfully follow
the promptings of the
Holy Ghost in all
that we do.

When we have
faith in the power
of Christ to save us
from our sins, we will
be profoundly motivated
to live in accordance with
His will. The Holy Ghost will
bless each of us with eternal
perspective. We will not only
believe in Christ, but we will
also believe Christ, with the
quiet spiritual confirmation
of our celestial potential.
We will also be blessed
to know that we are
the work of His
hands.

Those
with adulterous
hearts seek signs to
satisfy a carnal curiosity
that requires a greater and
greater intensity of validation,
that they might achieve the same
degree of gratification, which is
nothing more than theological
titillation. In the scriptures,
such individuals are aptly
described as being past
feeling.

If we want to enjoy the gift of the Holy Ghost, we must "let go and let God." Only then will we catch a religious fever that spikes the temperature of our testimonies, and gets us going by warming up our faltering faith.

When we
feel the energy
of the Holy Ghost
building within us, we
realize that it can lift us
to the zenith of experience,
until the lines distinguishing
mortality from eternity blur.
At that moment, when we find
ourselves in a condition that,
for the lack of better words,
can only be described as if
we were being born again,
we will be consumed in
a fire of everlasting
burnings.

Some recognize the Holy Ghost as nothing but our intuition, which is our capacity to understand something without the need for conscious reasoning.

The Hubble telescope
can "see" 13.2 billion light
years into our past, almost to
the moment of creation itself,
but it cannot gaze into heaven
for five minutes, which thing
is easy for even children to
do, as long as they are
cast under the spell
of the Spirit.

The
Spirit
introduces us
to a ladder that
has been set up on
the earth, the top of
which reaches all
the way up to
heaven.

All of us are repeatedly faced with occasions when withdrawals must be made from our spiritual bank accounts. When we respond to the Spirit, Who drives us to our knees to help us to recognize the awesome power of the Atonement, we put the principle of repentance to its ultimate test. But we do not write checks that can't be cashed. We realize that only after regular deposits have been made over a period of time, can we rely upon the cornucopia of comfort created by the cushion of confidence that is a currency flowing from conduct that is consistent with the core curriculum of contrition.

The cataracts that are created by our concessions to sin cloud our vision. Our narrow perspective forces us into making comfortless compromises, leaving the landscapes of our lives as nothing more than empty vistas. If we do not take advantage of the therapy that is offered by the Holy Ghost, the prognosis must remain poor. He is a heavenly optometrist for eyes that have lost the ability to see clearly, and that can no longer make the distinction between good and evil and between light and darkness, and even between pleasure and pain. He can restore our vision to 20:20 acuity.

Armed with the
power that stems
from the Holy Ghost,
our innermost longings
to apprehend visions of the
eternal world are epitomized
by our triumphant realization of
dreams fulfilled. In the expression
of our testimonies, our emotions are
painted by words that depict our
progression toward the distant
mileposts that mark the way
we must all follow as we
journey on, in faith,
toward heaven.

When we walk in
the light of life and
we go out of our way to
grasp the principles of truth,
we brim over with gratitude as
we discover how our Redeemer has
provided luxurious accommodations
for us in the household of faith by
assigning us a room with an
unobstructed view of the
Holy Ghost.

The
Holy Ghost
helps us to have
bowels that have been
moved to compassion for
those who are struggling
with misfortune or the
heavy weight of
sin.

We can be fully committed and still have special moments of reconfirmation, when the Spirit works so powerfully upon us that we can say that our hearts have been changed through faith on the name of Christ, that we have been born of Him, and that we have become His Sons and daughters. We no longer have the disposition to do evil, but to do good continually.

We should never be so bold as to question the power of our Exemplar, or Jesus Christ, or of the Spirit, Who abides with us and is our Comforter.

If we have
never made the
journey to Christ,
if we have chosen not
to travel the path leading
to the Tree of Life, if we have
not worked diligently to harvest
the delicious fruit of that tree,
we cannot receive the things
of the Spirit of God, for
they will seem foolish
in our eyes.

Always looking
for the easy way out
condemns us to negotiate
the instability of the shaky
ground of telestial turf,
as opposed to the solid
footing that Gospel
sod offers to those
who put their trust
in the Holy
Ghost.

Ignorance is not bliss, but is rather, an element of enslavement. We all need the Light of Christ and the Holy Ghost to guide us.

We are more
than the sum of
our somatic senses.
The activation of our
spiritual sixth sense is
the key to our discovery
of undreamed of vistas of
otherwise inaccessible
experience.

We take for granted
that prophets, seers, and
revelators receive revelation.
But isn't it wonderful when the
sound of the voice of the Lord
that is so familiar to them is
for us a continuous melody
and a thunderous
appeal?

The Holy Ghost encourages us to vividly role-play, as well as to pre-play and re-play the lines we have been asked to deliver in the theater of life. It gives us the tools we need to be worthy understudies to the Star of the production, Who is our Lord and Savior Jesus Christ.

The Spirit stands ready to guide us unerringly, that we might know for ourselves the truthfulness of all things. Even more, as it molds and shapes us into new creatures in Christ, pure intelligence will flow unto us as the dews of Carmel.

One among many of the responsibilities of the Holy Spirit is to bear a sacred witness of our honesty with God and Christ as we repent with broken hearts. His justification is as a baptism of fire that puts the finishing touches on the Atonement of the Savior. Because Mercy intervenes to satisfy the demands of Justice and cancel the penalties that are associated with our sins, we are blessed to become holy and without spot, in a rite of purification. Though our "sins be as scarlet, they shall be as white as snow. Though they be red like crimson, they shall be as wool." (Isaiah 1:18).

It will be difficult for those who have lived a telestial existence to justify their behavior before God, in the face of the many signs and wonders He has revealed as both warnings and blessings. Those of us who have witnessed any or the least of these have seen God moving in his majesty and power.
(See D&C 88:47).

It is not easy for those who have turned their backs on the gifts of God to obtain forgiveness. Those who have not allowed Christ into their lives, "die in their sins, and they cannot be saved in the Kingdom of God." (Moroni 10:26).

Revelation may be recognized only when we have allowed ourselves to fall under the influence of the Spirit. Our acceptance of communication from the heavens waits upon our initiative. It is not subject to amendment, to our private interpretation, or to scrutiny by others.

The Spirit grounds us, not on telestial turf that is soiled with the stain of sin, but on broad celestial boulevards that have been paved with shining bricks of 24 carat gold. Truly, God dwells in everlasting burnings.

Our
divine
tutorial
training is
a process and
not a point.
That is just
how God
wants
it to
be.

We are intertwined
with Heavenly Father, Jesus
Christ, and with the Holy Ghost,
in palpable connections. They notice
when sparrows fall from trees, and on
cold winter nights, they help us to notice
the explosion of supernovas in distant
galaxies. They do not play dice with
Their creations; We can be sure that
They will leave nothing to chance.
We can be at-one with them
in every conceivable
way.

As the seasons
of our lives unfold
before us, we realize how
much we need the influence of
the Holy Ghost, for "life is a sheet
of paper white, where each of us may
write a line or two, and then comes
night. Greatly begin! If thou hast
time for but a line, make that
sublime. Not failure, but
low aim, is crime."
(James Lowell).

The Lord selects those
who are humble and worthy,
and then He tutors them through
the power of the Holy Ghost, revealing
His will unto them. Those whom He selects
are "the weak things of the world." (D&C 1:19).
As President Kimball once stated: "Christianity
did not go from Rome to Galilee. It was
the other way around. In our day, the
routing is from Palmyra to Paris,
and not the reverse."

The prophet Joseph Smith understood the influence of the Holy Ghost, when he prayed: "Help us by the power of thy Spirit, that we may mingle our voices with those bright, shining seraphs around thy throne, with acclimations of praise, singing Hosanna to God and the Lamb!" (D&C 109:79).

When
they do not
feel the power
of the Holy Ghost,
the children of men
can get caught in a
flat spin from faith,
from which recovery
can be extremely
difficult.

The Holy Ghost is a powerful financial ally Who can provide over-draft protection as we invest in the theater of life. He stands as a guardian. He is the custodian of our assets Who makes sure that the checks we are writing have been co-signed by Jesus Christ, so that they may later be cashed by a creditor who goes by the name of Justice, when our debts become due and payable.

We live in the
midst of Spiritual Babylon,
and recoil as we encounter the
sprawling wasteland of worldliness
that reeks of the rotting stench of sin.
The Holy Ghost cannot be dragged down
to its level, however, for He would never
allow Himself to be contaminated by
the raw sewage that is unleashed by
the servants of Satan, who often
try to disguise themselves as
sanitation workers.

Those who
were denied the
chance in this life to
embrace the Gospel will be
judged according to their more
limited understanding of the doctrines
and principles of God's Plan. Therefore,
when they approach the Bar of Justice, they
will necessarily vary in their accountability
to law. Therein lies the hidden power of the
Holy Ghost to ultimately bless their lives.
Beside the Savior, He will become their
advocate, and He will justify them
as long as their behavior had
been in harmony with the
principles of The
Plan.

Once we
have received the
anointing of the Holy
Ghost, we will not be able
to rest "until the last enemy
has been conquered, death
is destroyed, and truth
reigns triumphant."
(Parley P. Pratt).

The Spirit
teaches us about
the autobiographical
thread within each of us
that leads all the way back to
heaven. The Holy Ghost helps
us to remember that we have
been placed on the earth
precisely because it is
a machine for the
making of
gods.

If we want to develop the faith to choose the harder right, instead of the easier wrong, we must begin by taking a few confident steps into the darkness. Only then will the spiritual strong searchlight of the Holy Ghost illuminate the way before us.

Those with
the faith to choose
the harder right are like
"brave Horatius, the Captain
of the Gate," who declared: "To
each of us upon this earth, death
cometh soon or late. And how can
we die better, than facing fearful
odds, for the ashes of our fathers
and the temples of our gods?"
Here was a man who trusted
his relationship with
the Holy Ghost.

Faith
exposes us
to a constant
stream of insight,
intuition, inspiration
and revelation that flows
from above in a cascade of
creativity. A divine direction
dictates that we walk along
illuminated pathways as we
exercise our faculties of
mind and spirit.

The account of the creation that was written by Moses provided only the details that relate to the Fall of Adam and Eve, and to the Atonement of Christ, which is the doctrine that the Holy Ghost will help us to understand in order for us to develop the faith to live abundantly and to become heirs of salvation.

At the most basic level, idleness is the devil's workshop, and so our refusal to exercise the gift of the Holy Ghost is sin. It is wasting our precious resources in fruitless pursuits, when we should have been engaged in other and better quests for which we could have been blessed with the Spirit of God.

The faithful keep their faces oriented toward the light, so the shadows will always be behind them. Because of the Holy Ghost, they may not even be aware of the encroaching darkness.

Among the
greatest virtues
we can have are a
well-trained mind, a
body to match, a love of
achievement, and the sweet
influence of the Holy Ghost.
Without these, life can be
nothing more than smoke
and mirrors, and we
grow old before
our time.

When a faithless society is weighed in the balances and is found wanting, it can all be traced to its spiritually bankruptcy on an institutional scale.

When the
Spirit withdraws
from those who exhibit
but little faith, they typically
throw up defensive dross that has
been designed to deflect, disrespect,
disregard, discourage, or disparage
the uncomfortably penetrating
question: "What think ye
of Christ?"

When we feel the urge to push the Lord's agenda, the Holy Ghost can be our labor coach, providing us with just the right amount of encouragement we need to successfully deliver our witness without being overbearing.

Guidance from above, that
comes to us in the form of spiritual
promptings and subtle impressions, is more
common that many would suspect. There are
powerful intuitive communicators that strongly
influence nearly all of us to push forward in
the direction of our dreams, toward a faith
to believe that blesses us with a greater
appreciation of the concern of the
Holy Ghost for each of us.

We
all need the
faith to use the
awe-inspiring skills
from that heaven-sent
journeyman who is the
Holy Ghost. He will help
us build the stages upon
which we will enact the
magnum opus that is
nothing short of
the drama of
our lives.

Far too many
of us, by seeking the
approbation of the world,
allow ourselves to be tossed
about as flotsam and jetsam
on the sea of life, never to
enjoy the sweet blessing of
spiritual centricity that
we could have enjoyed
had we established a
relationship with
the Spirit.

As
we endure
in faith, precious
emanations of familiar
and soothing oscillations
of energy will resonate from
within the limitless reserves of the
Spirit. These are selflessly shared by
the One who has promised to carry us
along on rolling waves of revelation
toward a shoreline of stability that
nurtures a more sure witness of
the Savior's divinity, no matter
what the tide may bring
in tomorrow.

When we think as
adults, and put away
childish things, we give
up, to a degree, the ability
to express ourselves naturally,
with unrestrained spontaneity.
Similarly, if we stop viewing
the world thru the influence
of the Spirit, we can lose
our joie de vivre.

It is the influence of the Holy Ghost that protects us from all of the worldly contaminants of our material prosperity, as well as from the temptation to fill space with telestial trinkets that can canker our souls if they are viewed or used unwisely.

With
the Spirit,
we are more
trusting and we
speak without guile.
We are more transparent
and less prejudicial. We have
fewer pretensions and are more
genuine. We are less prone to
rationalization and quicker
to forgive. We are grounded
in many ways that bestow
upon us a confidence
that others cannot
know.

The
Holy Ghost
encourages us
to try the virtue
of the word of God.
We do so, that we might
reap its rewards, and with
diligence, patience, and
long-suffering, harvest
the fruit of the Tree
of Life from its
low-hanging
branches.

It is in His divine omniscience, that our Heavenly Father has given us the gift of the Holy Ghost so that we may successfully confront the demons who play a role in the opposition in all things that is such an integral part of our experiences. In the fight or flight scenario, it is our faith that becomes the launch pad for the anticipated adrenaline rush that, in turn, prompts us to invite the influence of the Spirit, to carry us beyond our night terrors.

The Holy Ghost is
the watchful guardian of
those who have matriculated
in the curriculum of the Gospel
but cannot sustain saving faith, set
their sights too low, or who easily reach
watered-down objectives. They no longer
stretch themselves, and rarely venture out
of the comfort zones to which they have
retreated. They have little to show for
their consistently timid efforts that
deny the faith but have become
habitual.

Wo unto those who groan under darkness and under the bondage of sin. They squander precious resources groping about in a frantic but fruitless search for meaning in their lives. In short, they fail to appreciate the stabilizing power that could have been theirs if they had only sought out the soothing influence of the Holy Ghost.

Our capacity for decisive action has been designed so that it might increase over time, as we are guided by the discipline of the Holy Ghost.

The
influence of the
Holy Ghost asks us to
shun telestial temptations
that are so cunningly peddled
by the snake oil salesmen who have
set up shop in the great and spacious
buildings that dot the landscapes of
our lives and that pop up in the
most unexpected places, and
at the most inopportune
moments.

Some
explain the
intuition that
we receive from
the Holy Ghost as
déjà vu, that literally
means "already seen," in
order to emotionally deal
with the powerful impression
that, somehow, a current event
has already been experienced.
Truly, religious recognition is
just that, a re-cognition or
a re-knowing of what we
have already learned
in our pre-mortal
spiritual home.

The
tendency
toward turmoil
lies in wait to disrupt
the poise of those who
are pressing forward
in the light of the
Holy Ghost.

The Holy Ghost prepares us to move onward and upward along a steady course of progress without encumbering ourselves with the wobbly constraints of uncertainty that always lie in wait to mislead those of a timid constitution or a shaky testimony.

Those
who zip along
in the fast lane of
life can far too easily
blow right past the celestial
signpost that has been erected
by the Holy Ghost, that would
have alerted them to move
over into the exit lane
leading to heaven's
gate.

We trust
the Holy Ghost
because we have
discovered how our
disposition to draw upon
His power can be stimulating
and even enlightening.

Blind opposition, enmity, hatred, hostility, inflexibility, and intolerance are the raw manifestations of pride, but these are overwhelmed by the accommodation, charity, faith, approachability, hope, and sociability of those who respond to the promptings of the Holy Ghost.

The
Holy Ghost,
together with
angels in heaven,
hold their breath while
waiting upon the initiative
of those who are charged
with the responsibility
to provide a good
example to
others.

The
unrepentant are
argumentative. They
abuse their position and
exercise unrighteous dominion,
while the humble speak softly, seek
peaceful solutions, invite the Spirit to
guide them in their interpersonal
relationships, and acknowledge
their love of God and man
as the engine that drives
their behavior.

Angels will attend us as we repent: "For I will go before your face," promised the Lord. "I will be on your right hand, and on your left, and my Spirit shall be in your hearts, and mine angels round about you, to bear you up." (D&C 84:88). With such a promise, how could we think to turn our backs on such reinforcement, return to our wicked ways, and determine to go it alone, without the guidance of the Holy Ghost?

The Holy Ghost intuitively draws us close to divine characteristics that cause us to shrink from sin and even to think of it as repulsive.

The Devil's bribery stands in sharp contrast and in opposition to the blessings that follow obedience to the promptings of the Spirit.

No matter
that we may, for all
intents and purposes, be
dead weight, the Spirit has
the capacity to carry us until
we have been revitalized, and
can once again walk and
not be weary, and run
and not faint.

Standing in opposition to the light of the Spirit is a darkness that has the potential to cover the earth, and gross darkness the people. Without the influence of the Holy Ghost to intervene in our behalf by introducing us to the Atonement, we would be held captive by the source of that darkness, to rise no more. The Devil, who was a liar from the beginning, even now continues his efforts to foil The Plan by the substitution of his own counterfeit, unworkable alternative that would not require repentance or the Atonement. Fortunately, in the setting of the Council in Heaven, we could see through his deception. Because of the guidance of the Spirit, we still do today.

It is only because
of the uninterrupted
intervention by our Father
in Heaven, His Son Jesus Christ,
and the Holy Ghost, that mortality
may become the wonderful learning
center for the talented and gifted
that it was envisioned to be even
before the world was made.

In the world, there is an ever-present negative energy that influences us; and the promptings that come to us from the Holy Ghost, that bring us to our knees, are the only possible countermeasures. Its only stipulations are that we confess when we have, in any magnitude, embraced the opposites that lie before us, and that we immediately undertake the safety protocols required by repentance to bring us back to our heaven on earth.

As
our circle
of knowledge
expands under
the influence of
the Spirit within us,
so do the borders of
darkness. The more we
know, the more we need
to learn. It should do no
violence to our faith if we
realize that, with a greater
understanding of truth, we
will surely have additional
questions that we wish to
ponder, even those that
relate to the mysteries
of the kingdom.

The Holy
Ghost guides our
lives with a profound
influence and helps us to
nurture the tender feelings
that shape our faith
to believe.

Our
thoughts
and feelings
relating to the
Spirit stand revealed
as our innocent attempts
to yoke our emotions and
our spiritual intuitions
to language.

The Holy
Ghost is the
great equalizer,
no matter in what
exclusive ecclesiastical
country club we may hold
a membership, or upon what
narrow theological terrace
we may have paused to
catch our breath.

To
avoid the
fate of those who
greet the Gospel with
skepticism, and to insure
that our faith is animated
with energy, and so that
we will have no regrets,
we have been given
the gift of the
Holy Ghost.

At times, the Spirit arouses us to trust in our own instincts, that they might lead us, with a little inspiration, to the highlands of the morning.

One of
life's purposes is
to refamiliarize us
with the noble principles
that guided us through the
spiritual kindergarten years of
our pre-mortal existence. We are
blessed with the companionship of
the Holy Ghost to accompany us
during our reintroduction to
that more natural state
of harmony with
heaven.

Faithless souls
see things as they
are, and wonder "Why?"
The Holy Ghost inspires us
to dream things that never
were, and to ask "Why not?"
He blesses us with the vision
that we all need, to work
through our problems,
instead of working
around them.

An
unprincipled
and faithless society
deals with its spiritual
myopia with a knee-jerk
reaction that simply ratchets
down its expectations. In the
end, a culture that lacks the
guidance of the Spirit will
ask very little of its
members, and will
receive in
kind.

It is because of the
Sacrament, that, as fire in
the sky, the air in the theater of
life is charged with an electricity that
represents the inevitable merger of the
universal encouragement of the Light of
Christ with the guidance provided by the Holy
Ghost. Streaking in tandem across the heavens,
their trajectories coalesce to trace a flaming
trail that sparkles over a vast cosmic ocean
that is alive with energy. Over the ebb and
flow of its tide, God creates a bridge of
understanding between the secular and
the divine, that is buttressed by the
cohesive influence of the mighty
foundation of our faith.

In matters of faith, attitude is all about altitude. We must raise our sights, so that we will always be looking upward, in the direction of our Comforter, the Holy Ghost.

We find ourselves surrounded by the world, and without the stabilizing influence of the Holy Ghost moral equivocation can far too quickly become the easier way out, and, in time, define the pattern of our conduct.

The
Holy Ghost
allows us to see
beyond the limited
horizon of our sight,
to be touched by a vision
of the virtue of the word of
God. His power enables us to
savor revealed truth with a
discriminating taste that
discerns the distinctive
flavor of eternal
worlds.

"We speak, not in the words which man's wisdom teacheth, but which the Holy Ghost teacheth." (1 Corinthians 2:13).

When our minds
are locked on telestial
targets, and we even attempt
so-called higher level thinking
without the influence of the Spirit,
we risk becoming as sounding brass
and tinkling cymbals. Without the
Holy Ghost, we are hollow on
the inside and the echo of
silence is deafening
to our ears.

How fitting when our testimony meetings consist of our discreet expressions relating to the guidance we receive from the Spirit, that is beyond our limited understanding, and that helps us as we face challenges, as we make important decisions, and as we grapple with the greatest questions relating to our faith.

The enthusiastically ignorant attempt to drag communication from the heavens down to their level so that it is in harmony with their myopic view of life. The world ridicules revelation and disparages its delivery. But such feeble efforts ring hollow compared to the thunder, lightning, and burning bush of Sinai.

The way to comprehend the hidden treasures of knowledge is by pressing forward with dedication to feast upon the word of Christ. We thereby receive the physical and spiritual strength and nourishment that we need in order to righteously endure to the end with continuing responsibility and accountability. At all times, we are supported and sustained by the Spirit.

The gift of
the interpretation
of tongues may include
the ability to comprehend the
words of the scriptures, as well as
the inspired counsel that flows
from the lips of those who sit
in the presiding quorums
of the Church.

If we have
faith in the atoning
power of Christ, and if
we furthermore possess the
resolve to do whatever we must
to activate the spiritual energy that
is lying dormant within us, we will
profit by the administration of
the gifts of ministering angels
who appear before us in
bodily form.

Our resources
are largely focused
upon the programs that
nurture our familiarity with
the Holy Ghost. The bestowal
of spiritual gifts is the antidote
for poisonous telestial tendencies.
Like the noxious weeds that we may
overlook in a flower garden, our
tolerance of worldliness can
crowd out the expression
of celestial sureties.

It is one thing
for an ignorant people
to live in opposition to the
laws of God. However, it is quite
another for those who have had the
light, and who have enjoyed spiritual
gifts, to turn from them, willfully rebel,
and intentionally seek out darkness. To
do so is an abomination, because it
represents unfaithfulness to
the Bridegroom.

Professors of religion who have stepped out of the light that radiates from the Spirit are those who "teach for doctrines the commandments of men, having a form of godliness, but they deny the power thereof." (J.S.H. 1:19).

Before we commit to any difficult course of action, we make the issue a matter of prayer so that we may experience the confirming witness of the Spirit. When we receive fire for the deed, we cannot fail.

As we hone our revelatory capabilities, we can build upon experiences with the Spirit that we have already had, that include our testimonies of Jesus Christ and of His Gospel, of the divine authenticity of The Book of Mormon, and of the mission of Joseph Smith.

Personal revelation is at the foundation of the living, vital, quickened Gospel of Jesus Christ, and is a cornerstone of God's perfect Plan of Salvation.

The Plan
provides the
loom upon which
we busily weave the
complex tapestry of our
lives, as we create our own
coats of many colors. But central
to the vitalization and execution of
our efforts is detailed instruction that
comes from above, in the form of
personalized guidance from the
Master Tailor Himself, as well
as from His authorized
representative, the
Holy Ghost.

What we call "coincidence" is often simply our Heavenly Father Who is working behind the scenes. Every moment of our lives is influenced by His divine design. We just need to be in tune with the Spirit in order to recognize it and act upon it.

Truly,
when God
said: "Let there
be light," it was a
simple statement of
fact as much as it was
a command. It was an
invitation to recognize,
embrace, and celebrate
the light that dances
all around us in
a revelatory
rapture.

It is with a great
deal of empathy that the Holy
Ghost shares our perspective, but
He also sees thru the clarifying and
purifying lens of eternity. He blesses
our lives in many ways by nurturing our
understanding of The Plan of Salvation.
The veil that has been drawn before our
eyes only prevents us, for a moment,
from seeing eternity with His
unobstructed view.

A number of
the chapters in the
story of our lives have
already been set to type,
and we aren't sure how many
remain to be written. But this we
know: The fairytale was created by
Heavenly Father, and we must honor
its premise that we are His sons and
daughters. We cannot start over and
make a new beginning, but we can
begin now, and with the help of a
talented and gifted Ghostwriter
Whose real name is the Holy
Ghost, make a brand new
ending to our life's
adventure.

In marvelous ways,
the Holy Ghost confirms
the belief of Heber J. Grant,
who declared that as we gain
spiritual maturity and do our
duty, our faith will increase
"until it becomes perfect
knowledge."

If we
ignore the
influences of
the Light of Christ
and the Holy Ghost that
nurture our innate urge to
abhor mischief, but instead allow
ourselves to be habitually distracted
by trifling concerns, we sin by omission
and risk settling for life in a marshland
of mediocrity. We can quickly become
mired in the quicksand of sin, from
which there is no easy escape.

One of the
terrible consequences
of the fascination of Babylon
with telestial titillation, and with
its fixation on the vain images of
the world, is spiritual insensitivity
to the impressions it might have
received had it been even
remotely interested in
the Holy Ghost.

A tenet of faith
of The Church of Jesus
Christ of Latter-day Saints is that
its members believe in institutional and
personal continuing revelation that comes
from Heavenly Father through the medium
of the Holy Ghost. However, "looking
for the spectacular, we often miss
the constant flow of revealed
communication that comes."
(Spencer W. Kimball).

God
continues
to reveal many
great and important
things pertaining to the
Kingdom. He sends us tenderly
crafted "letters" of encouragement
hoping that we will receive and read
them with excitement. Open lines of
communication from the Spirit are
nurtured to become avenues of
correspondence that freely
flow between heaven
and earth.

No wonder that it is the priest's duty to preach, teach, expound, exhort, and to baptize, as well as to administer the sacrament. (See D&C 20:46). Their awesome responsibility is to speak with faith by the power of the Holy Ghost as if their voices were the Lord's, and then to follow up with action.

When we are
permitted to look
with the eye of faith
thru a spiritual prism,
we can see beyond the
limited horizon of our
sight, all the way into
eternity. Our eyes are
opened by the Spirit
to understand the
things of God.

Without the Spirit, there can be no faith; without faith, there can be no light, and without light there can be no recognition of religious truth; and without spiritual enlightenment, if just one of the three elements of faith, light, and truth is lost, then all must be forsaken. Our fortunes rest on the basis of how completely we have embraced the influence of the Holy Ghost.

Faith, light, and truth may be recognized as irreducible common denominators. They are the essential elements of an equation that describes the foundation upon which knowledge is received. "One for all and all for one!" was the motto of the Three Musketeers. Without faith, light, and truth, we would retrogress; we would degenerate from God, descend to the devil, and lose knowledge. If we do not have the knowledge of the Spirit to be with us, we cannot be saved.

When, by faith, we are infused with the knowledge of God, our bodies are filled with light, and there is no darkness in us. We comprehend all things. (See D&C 88:67).

Our faith pushes us toward perfection, which often means that we persevere to the point that we feel that we have no more to give. It is at the point of utter exhaustion that we cast our burdens on a power that is greater than ourselves, even on the Holy Ghost, if we hope to be able to survive the ordeal.

Telestial
E.M.T.s are at a
total loss for diagnosis,
while the supernal gift of the
Atonement provides a virtual war
chest of therapies for cold, stony,
and hard hearts. Our faith in the
merits of Jesus Christ is the
remedy of choice for
reconciliation.

The
attention
and adoration
of the world is a
satanic seduction to
influence us to abandon
the Holy Ghost and leave
our coats of many colors
hanging unattended and
unused in the back of
our closets.

If we would just let the Holy Ghost do His job, we would have less trouble sleeping, less difficulty focusing, and less of a problem concentrating on the principles of the Gospel.

In every age,
the tender shoots of
young testimony spring up
and are carefully nurtured in
accordance with Alma's inspired
formula. Our understanding comes
from the Spirit of Truth, without the
ecclesiastical embroidery that too
often needlessly complicates the
simple sewing, and sowing, of
Gospel doctrine and its
related principles.

As long as we remain in a
state of rebellion against the
Spirit, the fruit of the Tree of Life
must remain just beyond our reach,
even if, for the sake of curiosity, we
now and then would like to take a
bite. If we never raise our eyes to
search eternal horizons, the world
before us will appear as nothing
more than a barren desert that
is devoid of refreshing oases,
the welcome shade of trees,
and an abundance of well
watered gardens. If we
lack faith to nourish
the word, not even
its living water
can sustain
us.

Our testimony of the truth includes three essential elements. At first, we are introduced to an eternal principle. Second, is our correct understanding of the Lord's counsel concerning the principle, and finally, is our experience with the principle, that is accompanied by the sure witness of the Spirit.

Faith is impotent when it does not lead to purposeful performance. It is the sizzle without the steak. Real faith involves a vital, personal self-commitment to a practical belief. But in the end, even our belief will ring hollow if it lacks the confirming witness of the Holy Ghost.

We are imperfect mortals who are struggling to believe what we do not see. The reward of our maturing faith is to see what we believe. Some things just have to be believed to be seen. Faith activates our desire to know by the witness of the Holy Ghost.

During the
genesis of our faith, it
is necessary for us to take
a few steps into the darkness,
in order to let the spiritual strong
searchlight of truth illuminate the
way. Only after the trial of our
faith will it be confirmed by
the Spirit that God is both
both its Author and its
Finisher. He has us
covered, both
coming and
going.

The
light of the
Spirit gives every
thread in the fabric of
our own faith a vitality,
vim, vigor, and vivacity that
is unique to holy vestments.
Their steadfast colors will
never fade, except through
neglect or unbelief. They
will remain impervious
to blemishes, but for
the stubborn stains
of unresolved
sin.

The
Holy Ghost
would never think
to pay the exorbitant
price of admission to the
amusement parks of Babylon.
Instead, He urges us to utilize the
aid stations providentially positioned
all across Zion, and that are free to the
public. Faith, repentance, and baptism are
costs that have been paid in advance, and
that thereafter take the form of a weekly
annuity that we receive each time we
partake of the Sacrament.

The Holy Ghost is the best fitness trainer we could ever have. But His performance requirements do ask us to expend soul-sweat. As Robert Frost reflected: "I shall be telling this with a sigh somewhere ages and ages hence: Two roads diverged in a wood, and I took the one less traveled by, and that has made all the difference."

In harmony
with the principle
of opposition in all
things, an impenetrable
veil has been drawn across
our minds. But we have the Light
of Christ, and the unimpeachable
witness of the Holy Ghost, to assist us
in our efforts to probe that mysterious
curtain. In the interim, many of us are
swayed by the siren song of Satan, drawn
to the duplicitous shoals of his spiritual
instability, thereon to founder, and
to be pulled under by the riptides
of religious relativism and the
undertow of agnostism, or
faithless skepticism.

Because of
the Holy Ghost,
we are honest, true,
chaste, benevolent, and
virtuous. Our concern for
others is more genuine,
and our hope relies
more heavily on
our faith.

If we
allow ourselves
to succumb to fear,
and permit faithlessness
to handcuff the expression
of our actions, often all that is
left in the end is a monochromatic
and a one-dimensional compromise
that can leave us with a hollow core
of emptiness deep in the pit of our
stomachs and the pounding thump
of terror in our hearts. Our faith
remembers to say its prayers,
and it never forgets to
ask for the Spirits'
intervention.

The Holy
Ghost commits
us to the arduous
process of spiritual
rebirth that accompanies
choosing the harder right,
rather than capitulating to
the character-crippling
miscarriage of the
easier wrong.

The gentle
nudging by the Holy
Ghost provides us with the
regularly recurring reassurance of
a recalibration of our priorities that
auto corrects with a celestial precision.
He envelops us in an intuitive appreciation
of where we came from, why we are here, and
where we are going. He gives us the courage
to face the future with confidence and
to maintain our forward momentum
during the journey so we won't
lose our balance, fall down,
and possibly injure our
sensitive divine
nature.

Our
faith charges
the atmosphere in
the theater of life, as if
it were fire in the sky, with
an electricity that represents the
inevitable merger of the universal
encouragement of the Light of
Christ with the pointed and
providential guidance of
the Holy Ghost.

Our attempts
to comprehend the
universe may help us
to understand ourselves.
If we ask, what is its origin,
or what is its ultimate destiny,
we are really asking where did we
come from, and where are we going.
When we discover the answers to these
questions, we will understand why we
are here, and we will be prepared to
embark upon a journey where our
traveling companion is the Holy
Ghost. With Him as our Guide,
it will become a pathway of
faith into the future.

Even with the aid of
the world's most powerful
telescopes, and notwithstanding
the Light of Christ, we have been
privileged only to take a peek
at the creations Moses beheld
through the power of faith
and under the mighty
influence of the
Spirit.

While they drew, a kindergarten teacher walked up and down the rows in her classroom, observing her pupils' work. She stopped at the desk of one little girl and asked what her drawing was. She replied: "I'm drawing a picture of God." The teacher paused, and then hesitantly said: "But no one knows what God looks like." Without looking up, the girl said: "They will in a minute." Though tender in years, this little child was responding to the sweet influence of the Holy Ghost.

When the Spirit nurtures our eternal focus of faith, we will "discard the poor lenses of our bodies, and peer through the telescope of truth into the infinite reaches of immortality." (Helen Keller).

The Holy Ghost asks a lot of us. However, in return, He emboldens us with hope, and He will bless us with the fortitude to endure. He motivates us to seek after everything that is lovely, or of good report, or praiseworthy.

Wo unto those who
only casually receive the
illumination of faith in God
that has been so generously given
by the Holy Ghost. Because of their
misguided obsession with temporal
trivia, they carelessly fritter away
their faith, and waste the days of
their probation rooting through
telestial trash in a fruitless
effort to provide substance
and to find meaning in
their empty lives.

By allowing
ourselves to be
habitually distracted
by trifling concerns until
they become the center of our
attention and even our obsession,
we ignore our innate yearnings to
exercise faith in God that comes
to us as a gift of the Spirit.
Thereby, we commit a
grievous sin of
omission.

When we deny
the gifts of the Spirit, our
equilibrium becomes disoriented,
and our moral compass spins out of
control. Too often, we hastily adjust
our values in a misguided and vain,
but surprisingly intuitive, attempt
to regain a state of balance
with the light of Christ,
the Holy Ghost, and
the heavens.

In a
vain attempt
to avoid societal
implosion, and for
the sake of cultural
expediency, the target has
been moved so many times
to score repetitive bulls-eyes,
that no-one will concede that
it is the arrow of faith that
has strayed far from the
mark because it lacks
guidance from the
Holy Ghost.

When we
no longer believe,
the compromise of our
conversion can be attributed
to a lack of faithful focus that
initiated the flat spin from which we
could not recover. The blame for the
demolition of our discipleship and
the chain-reaction of unfortunate
and inevitable consequences that
follows is too often laid at the
doorstep of others, while it
is we who have lost the
orientation of the
Holy Ghost.

The faithful find mentors whom they can emulate, instead of scapegoats that are easy to blame. Instead of looking for easier answers, the Spirit invites us to dig deeply, to discover better solutions.

As the process of our conversion unfolds, we slowly become aware of the divine design that has been mapped out for all of us. "Our lives are fairy tales waiting to be written by the finger of God." (H.C. Anderson).

The activities
in which the unfaithful
are engaged do not require
commitment to a belief, but only
minimal effort, little responsibility, and
virtually no accountability. Someone once
said that the Lord gave us two ends: one to
think with and the other to sit on. Which one
we use will determine how well we do in life.
In other words: Heads we win, and tails we
lose. But it's always nice to have a little
help from our friends, beginning with
our greatest benefactor, Who is
the Holy Ghost.

Our
best intentions
may be noble, but
work without vision
is drudgery, and even
if we have vision, without
work, it is dreamery. If we
focus our faith and work with
vision, however, if we work in
tandem with the Holy Ghost,
it will be our fortune to
soar among eagles,
rather than walk
with turkeys.

The
Holy Ghost
pushes us beyond
our normal capacity
and instills within us
a quiet resolve to
lengthen our
stride.

We know
that our weaknesses
are among the fibers that
have been woven by God into
the fabric of our lives. We simply
turn to the inventory of thread that
is provided by the Holy Ghost, that
enables us to weave new patterns
that reflect the celebration
and expression of our
faith.

The
Holy Ghost
encourages us
to constantly strive
to do more, to be better,
to seek understanding, and
to empower ourselves with the
blessing of wisdom. We emulate
the motto of Olympians, which
is "Citius, Altius, Fortius,"
or "Faster, Higher,
Stronger."

The Holy Ghost "generates power, for a mind once stretched by a new idea can never return to its original dimension." (Oliver Wendell Holmes).

The Spirit
provides a way
for us to increase our
metaphysical metabolism, to
target the fat of faithlessness
when our hearts are broken.
Time is the fire in which we
burn away the calories of
contrition in the fiery
hot crucible of
faith.

The
celestial compass
of the Spirit is calibrated
to be oriented toward truth,
and is always available to guide
the faithful to a safe haven. It is also
there for those who have lost their way,
to bring them into the fold of the Good
Shepherd, or to show them how to return
to the security of the community of
Christ from which they have
strayed.

Those who have not
bothered to invest the time
to get to know the Holy Ghost
simply lack spiritual horsepower.
Their dearth of traction is obvious,
their inability to generate spontaneity
is palpable, and their lack of energy
to engage enthusiasm is noticeable.
Their incapacity to spark vitality
is evident, and their failure to
candidly acknowledge the
powerful relationship that
can exist between them-
selves and the Spirit
is undisputed.

The level
of our faith
must be elevated
to something more
dynamic than a simple
mechanical observance
of a multiplicity of
ceremonial rules.
The Holy Ghost
personalizes
the Plan.

The Holy
Ghost steps
up and helps
us, as we catalyze
our feeling, capture
our emotion, contour
our attitude, crystallize
thought, congeal passion,
compartmentalize action
and convey sentiment,
that lead to spiritual
revitalization.

The
Holy Ghost
provides us with
the regularly recurring
reassurance of a religious
recalibration that autocorrects
with fortuitous frequency and
with celestial precision. He is
always waiting in the wings
to assist us if we stumble
or have forgotten the
lines we had earlier
memorized in the
Three Act Play
of the Plan.

The
Holy Ghost
stimulates soul-sweat
as it works on our sense
of duty, our conscience,
and our scruples, to
quietly nurture our
faith to believe.

The Holy Ghost envelops us in an intuitive appreciation of where we came from, the tangible element of why we are here, and the revelatory reassurance of where we are going.

The Holy Ghost
endows us with fluency
in a heavenly language that
is rhythmical, melodious, and
soothing to our ears. It is calming
to our souls. When we hear the Spirit
quietly whisper: "You're a stranger
here," we are comforted by the
reassurance that all of us
have "wandered from a
more exalted sphere."
(Eliza R. Snow).

The Holy
Ghost prompts
us to examine what
it means to be anxiously
engaged, inspires us to plumb
the depths of our commitment to
the Savior, sensitizes us to the nobility
of His work, expands upon His visions of
immortality, personalizes the Atonement,
and helps us to remain consciously
aware of our close proximity
to heaven.

From the inexhaustible resources of the Holy Ghost, we receive streams of inspiration and revelation that cascade down from above. This insures that our walk along illuminated pathways will lead to the only institution that may legitimately claim inspiration from divine guidance.

The Holy
Ghost prompts
us to examine what
it means to be anxiously
engaged, inspires us to plumb
the depths of our commitment to
the Savior, sensitizes us to the nobility
of His work, expands upon His visions of
immortality, personalizes the Atonement,
and helps us to retain a remission of
our sins and to remain consciously
aware of our close proximity
to the angels in heaven.

The Holy Ghost is a nursemaid to the nations. He ministers by the power of faith. He uses His resources to reach out and lift up the downtrodden, no matter in which far corner of the earth they might be struggling.

Those of us who listen to the promptings of the Holy Ghost view afflictions, trials, and tribulations in a new light, and determine to discover how they might work to our benefit.

We must
venture forth
out of the shadows,
relying upon the guidance
that we receive from the Spirit,
as well as from the ministering of
angels, if we want to experience
the special familiarity that the
faithful enjoy with the Lord
of all the earth.

The more we think about Christ, the easier it is to craft in words the sensations that naturally flow to us, as a result of the stirrings of the Spirit. It becomes less difficult to generate and to sustain the faith to believe in the Father, the Son, and the Holy Ghost.

The Holy Ghost will bless us to be able to feel the gentle caress of the Master's hand, as our spiritual muscles are massaged by faith. We want Him to mold us and shape us as the Artisan of our destiny.

We are enveloped by the Spirit in a shower of divinely directed diamond dust that glitters with thousands of points of light that are nothing short of reflections from above.

The cohesive
influence of the
Spirit creates a bridge
of understanding between
the secular and the divine.
Life, with all its twists and
turns, and its permutations
and combinations, suddenly
makes more sense, as we
begin to understand
the mind and will
of God.

The
Holy Ghost
sustains us as
we receive with
equanimity whatever
comes our way during
the incubation period of
our spiritual metamorphosis
that was designed to be just
as challenging as it would
be rewarding.

The Holy Ghost
never fails to surprise
us in myriad and delightful
ways with His quiet influence. He
cultivates a culture of reflection,
keeps the Savior in our thoughts,
nurtures an eternal perspective,
initiates positive change, and
helps us to harmonize our
behavior with heaven's
code of conduct.

We
watch ourselves
judiciously, and are
the meticulous guardians
of our thoughts, the scrupulous
custodians of our words, and the
prudent caretakers of our actions.
We fastidiously observe the laws of
God, that we might benefit from the
stability of a pathway that basks in
the steady illumination that is
generously provided by the
quiet influence of the
Holy Ghost.

When we
are hesitantly
inching our way thru
life, the Spirit invigorates
us with renewed energy, and
instills within us the desire
to redouble our efforts to
maintain the integrity of
our testimonies.

Who would
consciously choose to
lead a marginalized life, or
to become spiritually depleted
on a personal or an institutional
level? We perish because our faith has
failed us. But how many of us have the
courage to realize that it is really the
other way around; that it is we who
have failed our faith? Fortunately,
if we are blessed with the gift
of the Holy Ghost, we can
change all that, starting
right now.

We do not want to
be spiritually starved,
doctrinally dehydrated,
or intellectually inhibited
while only inches away from
the source of truth that could
have satisfied our hunger, and
from the stream of continuous
insight, intuition, inspiration,
and revelation that freely
flows from the source
of all truth, even
the Spirit.

The Holy Ghost carries us in positive and meaningful ways to green pastures where we enjoy the warm embrace of the Good Shepherd, and where we are permitted to experience the intimacy of the touch of His garment, even if we sometimes feel that we are lost in the press of the crowd within the sheepfold.

The Holy
Ghost ignites our
souls with passion. It is His
catalyzing influence that was
conspicuously missing from the
pedantic charade of righteous
behavior that was embraced
by the Pharisees of old,
and that is found in
so many circles
even today.

As we
rehearse
in our minds
the expression of
our witness that Jesus
is our Savior, it is with our
faith that we hear the music
of a celestial symphony that
has been scored for every
imaginable instrument.
In the repertoire of
the Holy Ghost,
there is music
for every
ear.

The Spirit helps to reacquaint us with a divine design as we put the finishing touches on our dissertation on life. As it is perfected, our composition will be recognized for what it has become: A true magnum opus, even God's work and glory.

Those who enjoy the fruits of faith, consecrate their lives to the Savior, They throw themselves on His altar of sacrifice, whose foundation is buttressed by a supernal display of divine direction that flows out of the Holy Ghost.

The
Holy Ghost
nudges us off
our complacency
plateaus, as we steer
away from the trendy
cafés situated along the
broad avenues of Idumea.
As upon the wings of eagles,
we are transported beyond the
boundaries of self-imposed
limitations along another
highway that leads
to heaven.

By
the Spirit,
we are caught
up in a rapture
where we can almost
hear legions of angels
who confirm that the earth
has become "a machine for
the making of gods."
(Henri Bergson).

In order to return to our home in heaven, we must be able to enjoy the sweet companionship of the Spirit as do our little children.

Adults who have learned to swim with sharks are characterized as "seasoned veterans" and yet the process fails to tenderize them. Instead, it curses them with a thick skin containing precious few sensory nerve endings that leave room for the gentle whole body massage that we sense as the nurturing influence of the Holy Ghost.

If we fail to nurture the tempering influence of the Spirit, we will strangle ourselves with material things whose opacity obstructs our ability to see how God has so thoughtfully laid out before us the smorgasbord of life, and has invited us so generously to freely partake of its delights.

It is the Holy
Ghost that purifies us
from caustic influences,
and decontaminates us from
the toxicity that is so prevalent
in the world. It neutralizes the
homogenization process that
can occur as we are tossed
about by the vagaries
of life.

The
Holy Ghost
is not a calorie
counter. He is thrilled
when we feast upon
the words of
life.

The Spirit extends to us the promise of a wonderful opportunity to enjoy the bliss of His abode in heaven. It is there that, ultimately, we will delight in the warm embrace of Heavenly Father, His Son Jesus Christ, and the Holy Ghost.

The
Spirit of God
selflessly moves us
past dependence and
beyond independence, to a
stimulating and interdependent
relationship with our Father in
Heaven and Jesus Christ. As a
facilitator, the Holy Ghost is
content to quietly work
behind the scenes in
our behalf.

Our
faith reflects
enduring qualities
that are the embodiment
of the nurturing influence of
the Holy Ghost. We see others as
neighbors and not as strangers.
We are less judgmental and
are more accepting of our
differences. We are less
suspicious and are
friendlier.

It is by the
power of the Spirit
that we fondly envision
the happiest place on earth.
We realize that if we return to
the childhood of our dreams, we
may be blessed to discover the
magical kingdom where they
will all come true.

No matter in what direction we face, we will always feel the presence of the Spirit, for it will be before us, forever and a day.

It is
because
of the Spirit
that we can rely
upon the horns of
sanctuary, to grasp
them whenever our
yoke seems too
heavy for us
to bear
alone.

If
we try
to shirk the
demands that the
Spirit places upon us,
we risk being swallowed
up by a leviathan no less
real than that experienced
by Jonah. We can then only
expect to be spit out upon
the white sandy beaches
of the obligations we
have made to
God.

Blessed are those who apprehend that our greatest battles are fought within the silent chambers of our souls.

Our
best intentions
may be noble, but
work without vision
is drudgery, and even
if we have vision, without
work, it is dreamery. If we
focus our faith and work with
vision, however, if we work in
tandem with the Holy Ghost,
it will be our good fortune
to soar among the eagles
in our lives, rather than
walk with the turkeys
who scratch out a
meager existence
along the way.

In the Standard Works, we are urged 129 times to learn, 154 times to be perfect, and 306 times to be obedient, but 995 times to begin. Now is the time that we must begin to cultivate a working relationship with the Spirit of God.

Because of
the influence of the
Holy Ghost, we will never
thirst, because He encourages
us to push our taproots down
thru Gospel topsoil until they
have reached a free, full,
flowing fountain of
living water.

The
Holy Ghost
knows how to
turn stumbling
blocks into stepping
stones. Crisis becomes
opportunity, and victory
is snatched from the jaws
of defeat. He has witnessed
how "change can come as a
flash of lightning and a clap
of thunder. The people shrink
in fear, but after the storm.
flowers will bloom."
("I Ching").

The Holy
Ghost proves that
darkness cannot be
carried into a lighted
chamber, and so we seize
every opportunity we can to
be enveloped in light. We have
learned to face the sunshine, so
the shadows will always be behind
us. Darkness will still exist, but its
companions that take the form of
fear and uncertainty will be out
of sight and out of mind.

The Holy Ghost welcomes the trials we face, and views them as nothing more than pop quizzes in the learning laboratory of life. The Spirit sees the bigger picture and He is more invested in preparing us for the final exam that will come for each of us soon after our mortal curriculum has been completed.

The Holy Ghost blesses us with an abundance of faith, even the faith to take risks. We break free from the safety nets, the comfort zones, and the ports of refuge to which the timid apprehensively retreat at the first sign of danger, to squeak out their lives as they scurry about from one shadowy sanctuary to another, in a flight from faith.

The Holy Ghost has fulfilled His mission when He has convicted us of our sins and we have turned to the Savior with full purpose of heart.

The Holy Ghost is a light bearer Who carries the torch of truth as a beacon to guide those who are having difficulty finding their own way home.

The Holy Ghost refuses to accept the mediocrity in our lives. Instead He strives to align our behavior and associate our faith to be harmonious with the revealed word and nature of God.

John F. Kennedy
famously declared:
"We choose to do things,
not because they are easy,
but because they are hard. Our
goals will serve to organize and
measure the best of our energies and
skills. Our challenges are those that we
are willing to accept, and that we are
unwilling to postpone, but that we
intend to win." That is well put,
but we must never forget that
it is the Holy Ghost Who
gives us fire for
the deed.

Real professors of faith hunger and thirst after righteousness, and they are filled with the Holy Ghost. They press forward with dedication, feasting on the scriptures. They receive physical and spiritual nourishment, and they endure to the end with continuing responsibility and accountability.

The
Holy Ghost
is here to step in
just as soon as we
recognize the positive
and pleasant aspects of
endurance. He encourages
us to develop and maintain
spiritually aerobic fitness,
that we might meet the
unwavering demands
of our discipleship
without fatiguing
our faith.

As we
profess our
faith, the Spirit
encourages us to
move onward, but
not in the press of a
rowdy mob that jostles
for position in the three
ring circus of telestial
trivialities, conceptual
cul-de-sacs, and
doctrinal dead
ends.

Modern scribes and Pharisees who have little or no faith omit the weightier matters of the law. They strain at a gnat, and swallow a camel. They appear to be righteous, but inside are "full of extortion and excess." (Matthew 23:25). Our righteous desire to so live that we are worthy of the constant influence of the Spirit of God, brings us closer to the Lord Jesus Christ, leaving no room for hypocrisy to creep into our lives.

Woven into the
fabric of The Plan
of Salvation is a Golden
Ticket that bears not only
our name, but also the name
of the Holy Ghost. It is freely
offered to each of us, that we
might claim the blessings of
heaven if only we endure
to the end in faith.

We
may choose to
endure without the
comfort of the Spirit,
but if we do so, we must
also accept the inevitable
negative consequences that
are tied to unresolved sin.
This makes our endurance
much more painful than
it would otherwise
have needed
to be.

The Spirit
allow us to
be tested and
tempted so that
we might be able
to show ourselves
and all the heavens
if we are willing and
able to demonstrate
the faith we need
to go the second
mile.

The more we are able to exercise our faith to comprehend the character of God, the more the Holy Ghost will teach us about how we fit into His divine design. We learn how faith can drive the law of the Gospel of Jesus Christ into our inward parts.

Those who have been card carrying members of The Church of Jesus Christ long enough to have experienced a liberal measure of temporal, spiritual, emotional, and intellectual symmetry, may sometimes ask our Heavenly Father why His Spirit allows the world to tug at them? Why is it that their faith in Christ is not yet perfect?

The second mile
of faith asks us to
forge a spiritual bond
with the Holy Ghost through
a demonstration of obedience
that is more expansive than was
the law of carnal commandments.
It requires the inter-dependency of
the greater law of the Gospel
of Jesus Christ.

When the Holy Ghost has blessed us with faith to go the second mile, our obedience is no longer inconvenient, and we experience the soul-expanding desire to more unreservedly labor in the traces beside the Lord our God.

When we are under the influence of the Spirit, we speak of principles in such a way that those of faltering faith are encouraged to take their first tentative steps toward commitment, while, simultaneously, more spiritually mature disciples, as they realize that present levels of performance are not acceptable, are inspired to lengthen their stride.

Sooner or later, every member of the Church falls under the spell of the Holy Ghost, Who admonishes them to run, and not just walk, to the end of their lives, as they seek new ways to build the Church and Kingdom of God on the earth.

The Holy Ghost is sensitive to our needs, because the effectual and fervent prayers of the righteous availeth much. In conformity to the laws of heaven, the faithful tap into and draw virtue from a life force that is the Spirit of God. When they have done so, they have figuratively reached out and touched the hem of the garment of the Savior.

Those who
are blessed with
the humility of faith
regard the Holy Ghost,
Who knows everything
there is to know and
dwells in heaven, in
reverential awe.

Those
who embrace
the Holy Ghost
are blessed with a
clear perspective of
the pattern of heaven
that is traced out by the
finger of God upon the
fabric of a telestial
tapestry.

We are
free to move
about the cabin,
but the Holy Ghost is
always available to offer
a safety demonstration, to
show us how to find shelter
within His protective influence,
to be shielded from unexpected
turbulence, and to be protected
from the suffocating storms of
devious doctrine that swirl all
around us. It is always best
to keep those safety belts
securely fastened, even
if we think we have
been assigned our
seat in economy
comfort, better
known as the
household
of faith.

Those who have partaken of the sweet, sustaining influence of the Holy Ghost have experienced the power of heaven that stems from love, in sharp contrast to the Machiavellian influences of lust and the unrighteous desire for dominion that typify the kingdoms of the earth.

Is it
easier
to throw
in the towel
and give up, and
harder to push on,
and continue the good
fight? Is it easy to settle
for average, and difficult
to become exceptional? The
Holy Ghost willingly accepts
these challenges in our behalf,
not because they are easy, but
precisely because they are
hard.

If we
only ask
Him to do so, the
Holy Ghost will step
in and help us to clearly
identify the fingerprints of
Satan, because they have been
smeared all over a plethora of
penurious programs, policies,
politics, and parties that do
little more than to promote
personal and provincial
proclamations relating
to plans that are
petty, at best.

After we have asked for His Spirit to be with us, the Holy Ghost will leave His signature in the form of a distinct afterglow from the eternal worlds. This betrays a subtle link between heaven and earth that is unmistakable.

With our invitation to do so, the Holy Ghost will caress our spirits with inexplicable images of religious recognition, that remind us of our noble birthright.

The Holy Ghost will bless us with a spiritual "sixth sense" that allows us to create order amid chaos and make sense of creation.

No matter how
wide the net is cast,
science cannot explain
the flickering shadows of
eternity that dance all around
us, as the forgotten features of
immortality are illuminated
for all to see, by the light
of the Holy Ghost.

The
spiritual
sixth sense with
which we are blessed
may just be the lowest
common denominator in
the theory of everything. The
influence of the Holy Ghost is
the grand unifying phenomenon,
and although it exists without
dispute, it defies explanation
on a chalkboard, as well as
within the algorithms of
a mathematical
equation.

Through
the workings of the
Holy Ghost and by the power
of our faith, we can see all the
way to heaven. We have the capacity
to be carried beyond the perceptible
and palpable confines of this world
to a place where boundaries are
blurred, and the barricade of
borders evaporates in a
flood of light.

When it is our turn to come face to face with eternity, it will be the Holy Ghost Who will participate in the transformation of our mortal clay into a more enduring substance.

The light
of the body
is the eye, and
when it is single
to the faith to see
into heaven above,
our elements will be
stirred by the warm
glow that emanates
from the presence
of God, even the
Holy Ghost. It
is that Spirit
which will
charm
us.

There will come a day for the faithful when the sun shall not go down, "neither shall the moon withdraw itself. For the Lord shall be their everlasting light." (Isaiah 60:20). The Holy Ghost will move from His supporting role, directly onto our center stage.

Because
of the influence
of the Holy Ghost,
both the heavens and
the earth are bathed in
celestial fire that is akin
to the background radiation
that still lingers from the
cataclysmic moment of
creation itself.

The Holy Ghost guides us with a star map that illuminates the path that leads to our promised inheritance. He simply blesses us with an endowment of radiant and unearthly power.

As we
ascend
the ladder
of faith rung
by rung, to be
only gradually
introduced to the
potency of the Spirit,
we will see lightnings
and mountains smoking,
and perceive the voices of
trumpets and thunderings
that speak in a language
that is inarticulate and
is yet irrefutable.

The
Spirit blesses us
with the knowledge
that mortality is only
a tiny fraction of a much
larger reality, and that our
perspective is faulty only
when we believe it
to be unique.

Every
time we worthily
partake of the bread and
water of the Sacrament, we are
powerfully strengthened, so that the
promises of heaven might be realized.
We invite virtue to garnish our thoughts
unceasingly. As our confidence builds,
the doctrine of the priesthood distils
upon our heads as the dews from
heaven, the Holy Ghost is our
constant companion, and its
guidance flows unto us
without compulsion.

The Spirit confirms our faith to see all the way to heaven, and responds to our inquiry: "O God, where art thou, and where is the pavilion that covereth thy hiding place?" (D&C 121:1).

The Spirit molds us in mortality, and establishes us in eternity. It is here that we obtain the promise that we will one day be encircled by heavenly smiles and enjoy the music of celestial symphonies.

With spiritual sensitivity to our needs, the Holy Ghost quietly whispers to us that when the time for our preparation has passed, the time for action has arrived.

Even
when the
Spirit influences
us, opposition must
still exist as the basis
of a matrix of mayhem,
within which the fiery darts
of the adversary will continue
to trace an incendiary
trail of disorder.

The Spirit generates faith, not fear. We are as Bagheera, the powerfully built black panther in "The Jungle Book," who confided to Mowgli the man-cub: "I had never seen the jungle. They fed me behind bars from an iron pan till one night I felt that I was Bagheera the Panther, and no man's plaything, and I broke the lock with one blow of my paw. and came away." (Rudyard Kipling).

It is the
fragmentation
of order in our lives
that creates the friction
that is necessary to fuel the
fire of the Spirit that warms
the world. One could say
that opposition actually
makes life possible on
strait and narrow
path.

Only if we
exhibit the moral
discipline to incorporate
into our behavior the steady
guidance of the Holy Spirit, will
we be able to recognize, address,
reverse, and erase with finality,
the imbalance in our lives.
That guidance will lead
us to the Atonement
of Jesus Christ.

The Holy Ghost doesn't measure us from our head to our toes, but from our heart to the sky. When He does so, telestial tape measures will not do.

The
Holy Ghost
drives an engine
whose normal operating
temperature is somewhere
between the hot reservoir of
the Son (sic) and the cold
reaches of outer space.

Allowing the Holy Ghost to release us from captivity permits us to see things as they really are, and to enjoy a lucidity that comes more from the heart than from the head.

The
gate may
be strait, and the
way narrow, but those
who accept the Holy Ghost
as their Guide will find that it
is within their capacity to travel a
path of progression, by threading the
eye of the needle and walking a fine
line past the seemingly unalterable,
unavoidable, and unstoppable
demands of disproportion.

If we
ignore the
celestial laws
that are the only
homing beacons that
are powerful enough to
penetrate the swirling mists
of darkness in our telestial
world, we have tacitly chosen
an alternative course leading
to our destruction, as we run
aground on rocky coastlines
of personal misfortune that
are bereft of the influence
of the Holy Ghost.

The effects
of sin are inevitable
and are inescapable, but
for the intercession, by our
faith, of the Atonement. The
Maker and Fashioner of the
universe must intervene by
engaging laws that restore
equilibrium, or all is lost.
The Holy Ghost exists to
help to restore that
state of balance
in our lives.

We
partake
of the Sacrament,
that we might be given
the tools we need in order
to lengthen our stride. In a
confrontation of principles with
values that may tear at the fabric of
the natural world, the Savior asks us
to exert ourselves with actions that
will surely stretch the limits of our
ability. But in the process, we will
find that there is, in the Holy,
Ghost, an unlimited source
of spiritual strength.

The Spirit becomes a celestial bridge that transports the righteous past the vicissitudes of life all the way to the steadiness of the kingdom of God that lies above the turmoil of confusion.

It is with
the eye of faith, or
from the vantage point of
the Holy Ghost, that we see
things more clearly, as if we
have escaped our mortal clay
with its confining limitations
that distort our perspective
and negatively twist our
attention inward, to
worldliness.

By venturing forth out of our comfort zones and moving forward with purpose, we enlarge the dimensions of our spiritual center, to make room for the Holy Ghost to dwell in our hearts.

To successfully
complete the course
curriculum of the Gospel
and graduate with high honors
from the school of hard knocks,
we must first have completed one
or two public speaking courses
before giving our language
to exhortation by the
power of the Spirit.

Those who have embraced the Holy Ghost are empowered to follow the yellow brick road with their heart, might, mind, and strength until they reach the Emerald City of Oz.

Adam and Eve fell that they and their posterity might be able to nurture the moral fiber that we recognize today as saving faith. They were given the gift of the Holy Ghost, that they might find that happiness which has always been prepared for the Saints of God.

It is not enough merely to have been given the gift of the Holy Ghost. If we coast to a standstill before we have made our way to the feet of the Savior, we are at risk of toppling over. Our forward momentum needs to be maintained if we are to keep our balance as we follow His footsteps.

Jesus encouraged us to give ourselves completely and without reservation, that we might enjoy a state of harmony with Him and synchronization with the eternities. He asked us to search without ceasing, that we might discover the power inherent within the gift of the Holy Ghost.

The Holy Ghost provides balance in a world that has become befuddled by weights and measures that are contaminated by the evidence tampering of the adversary.

Without the softening influence that is one of the blessings that comes to us from the Spirit, we tend to exhibit both hard hearts and stiff-necks. We are overtly and covertly rebellious. We lack the malleability and the pliability of those who humbly seek guidance from above.

Without the influence of the Holy Ghost, we tend to manifest hard hearts, stiff-necks, and are overtly and covertly rebellious. We lack the malleability and the pliability of those who humbly seek guidance from above.

Those who are enamored with themselves will never experience the mind and soul expanding epiphanies that we receive from the Holy Ghost.

Without
the influence
of the Holy Ghost, we
seek after signs. When we
are past feeling, we require a
greater and greater intensity
of stimulation to receive the
same level of temporal or
theological gratification.
What we have been
given is never
enough.

Even
if we hit
a new low after
we have committed
awful sins, if we repent
and trust in the awesome
ability of the Atonement to
bind up and heal our wounds,
we will be long suffering and
not falter in our faith. When
things seem that they could
be no worse, we are at our
best, because then we are
particularly sensitive to
the comfort that comes
thru the whisperings
of the Spirit.

As we listen to the Holy Ghost, the righteousness of our efforts will be revealed in spectacular simplicity and plainness. The walls of opposition to our purposeful repentance will crumble and fall away. In our efforts, the Spirit will comfort and succor us with the bread of life. As we journey through the harsh and unforgiving environment of mortality, seeking the Lord while He may be found, oases will spring up in the desert and living water will slake our thirst.

The Spirit fosters an
atmosphere of collaboration,
conciliation, and cooperation,
and encourages us to share our
resources with others in order
to find answers to our most
disturbing questions. Thus,
all things work to our
mutual advantage;
we are profited,
thereby.

Because
we faithfully
persist in the process
of repentance, the Spirit
will teach us how to become
engaged in fashioning defensive
weapons in the armory of thought.
It is with these tools that the Holy
Ghost will show us how to put
together a vast arsenal of
heavenly munitions, such
as faith, hope, and
charity, strength,
peace, and
joy.

If we repent, we never thirst, because we are anchored through Gospel topsoil into a fountain of living waters, because of our reliance upon the Spirit. Repentance might be the definitive expression of honesty with ourselves, with Heavenly Father, with the Savior, and with the Holy Ghost.

As we repent, we nurture our relationship with God and the Holy Ghost. We become the fashioners of our fortunes, even as we learn to rely upon reserves that are only found in Jesus Christ. We realize that these are greater than any we could ever hope to merit on our own.

As we learn to listen to the whisperings of the Holy Ghost, we exercise our ability to look past the telestial temptations of temporal trivia. We develop a will to adjust our perspective so that the achievement of our goals becomes the obsession of our faith.

Today, our society is in a self-destruct mode that, according to D&C 1:16, seeks "not the Lord to establish his righteousness, but every man walketh in his own way, and after the image of his own god, whose image is in the likeness of the world, and whose substance is that of an idol, which waxeth old and shall perish in Babylon, even Babylon the great, which shall fall."

Sooner or later, each of us must discover for ourselves that a line has been drawn in the sand. If we then act upon the promptings of the Holy Ghost to seize the power of the Atonement, we will generate a positive energy that will move us forward in the direction of our dreams. Those who have faith to rely upon the merits of Christ thru His sacrifice will be saved in the kingdom of God.

It is
our honesty
with ourselves and
with the Holy Ghost
that tests the mettle of
our convictions. Through
our repentance, we put our
money where our mouth is. We
have no proof until we act on
the basis of trust. Then, comes
the confirmation of the reality
as feelings of self-confidence
grow and purposeful actions
replace tentative overtures.
In effect, we let go
and let God.

It makes
very little difference
to our Father in Heaven
whether we are combating the
influences of the Seven Deadly
Sins, or the garden-variety of
transgressions that we commit
every day. The Holy Ghost
is always there to guide
us back to the strait
and narrow way.

One among many of the responsibilities of the Holy Spirit is to bear a sacred witness of our honesty with God and Christ as we repent with broken hearts. His justification is as a baptism of fire that puts the finishing touches on the Atonement of the Savior. Because Mercy intervenes to satisfy the demands of Justice and cancel the penalties that are associated with our sins, we are blessed to become holy and without spot, in a rite of purification. Though our "sins be as scarlet, they shall be as white as snow. Though they be red like crimson, they shall be as wool." (Isaiah 1:18).

It
is for
our benefit
that we become
acquainted with evil
as well as with good, with
pain as well as with pleasure,
with darkness as well as with light,
with error as well as with truth, and
with punishment for the infraction of
God's eternal laws, as well as with the
blessings that follow our obedience.
The Holy Ghost is always there for
us when things get rough during
these character-building
experiences.

About The Author

Phil Hudson and his wife Jan have 7 children and over 25 grandchildren. They enjoy spending time with their family at their cabin nestled in the Selkirk Mountains, on the shore of Priest Lake, the crown jewel of North Idaho. Phil had a successful dental practice in Spokane, Washington for 43 years, before retiring in 2015. He has an eclectic mix of hobbies, and enjoys the out of doors. He always finds time, however, to record his thoughts on his laptop, and understands Isaac Asimov's response when he was asked: If you knew that you had only 10 minutes left to live, what would you do?" He answered: "I'd type faster."

Phil received the inspiration to write this book while he and Jan were serving as missionaries for The Church of Jesus Christ of Latter-day Saints, in the Kingdom of Tonga. While there, they celebrated their 50th wedding anniversary.

Often, it
is only when
we have enrolled
in the graduate school
of hard knocks, and have
pre-paid the required tuition,
that we obtain the credits that
are earned by our obedience
to the promptings of the
Holy Ghost.

By The Author

Essays

    Volume One: Spray From The Ocean Of Thought
    Volume Two: Ripples On A Pond
    Volume Three: Serendipitous Meanderings
    Volume Four: Presents Of Mind
    Volume Five: Mental Floss
    Volume Six: Fitness Training For The Mind And Spirit

First Principles and Ordinances Series

    Faith - Our Hearts Are Changed
    Repentance - A Broken Heart and a Contrite Spirit
    Baptism - One Hundred And One Reasons Why We Are Baptized
    The Holy Ghost - That We Might Have His Spirit To Be With Us
    The Sacrament - This Do In Remembrance Of Me

Book of Mormon Commentary

    Volume One: Born In The Wilderness
    Volume Two: Voices From The Dust
    Volume Three: Journey To Cumorah

Doctrine & Covenants Commentary

    Volume One - Sections 1 - 34
    Volume Two - Sections 35 - 57

Minute Musings: Spontaneous Combustions of Thought

    Volume One
    Volume Two
    Volume Three

Calendars:

    In His Own Words: Discovering William Tyndale
    As I Think About The Savior
    Scriptural Symbols

Children's Books

    Muddy, Muddy
    The Thirteen Articles of Faith
    Happy Birthday

Doctrinal Themes

    The House of the Lord

A Thought For Each Day Of The Year

    Faith
    Repentance
    Baptish
    The Holy Ghost
    The Sacrament
    The House Of The Lord
    The Atonement
    The Plan of Salvation

Professional Publications

    Diode Laser Soft Tissue Surgery Volume One
    Diode Laser Soft Tissue Surgery Volume Two
    Diode Laser Soft Tissue Surgery Volume Three

These, and other titles, are available from online retailers.

Agency and opposition are always before us, and so the Spirit stands as a sacred sentinel, beckoning us to enter in at heaven's gate, to find the Rest of God.

Quid magis possum dicere?

www.ingramcontent.com/pod-product-compliance
Lightning Source LLC
Chambersburg PA
CBHW060508240426
43661CB00007B/953